TIPS HANDED DOWN FROM MY GRANNY

COOK CAULIFLOWER IN CHIP BASKET. NO NEED TO STRAIN AND IT COMES OUT WHOLE

BEFORE COATING FRITTERS WITH BATTER ROLL IN FLOUR. PREVENTS BATTER RUNNING OFF FRITTERS

WHEN DRYING SOCKS OR STOCKINGS INDOORS. PEG TO WIRE COAT HANGER

Good Housekeeping

TRADITIONAL KITCHEN HINTS AND TIPS

Good Housekeeping
TRADITIONAL KITCHEN HINTS AND TIPS

EBURY PRESS
LONDON

First published in 1998

1 3 5 7 9 10 8 6 4 2

Text © 1998 Random House UK Ltd or the National Magazine Company

First published in the United Kingdom in 1998 by Ebury Press
Random House, 20 Vauxhall Bridge Road, London SW1V 2SA

Random House Australia (Pty) Limited
20 Alfred Street, Milsons Point, Sydney,
New South Wales 2061, Australia

Random House New Zealand Limited
18 Poland Road, Glenfield, Auckland 10, New Zealand

Random House South Africa (Pty) Limited
Endulini, 5a Jubilee Road, Parktown 2193, South Africa

Random House UK Limited Reg. No. 954009

A CIP catalogue record for this book is available from the British Library.

ISBN 0 09 186092 X

Text design by Jerry Goldie
Cover design by Slatter-Anderson

Printed and bound in China by L. Rex

Contents

Introduction

*M*any things have changed in the kitchen over the years – microwaves, freezers and food processors were undreamed of by our grandmothers or great-grandmothers, but their knowledge is still a valuable source of information on good cake baking, pastry making, expert meat carving and efficient cleaning and mending. It is these pieces of knowledge that have been gathered together on the pages of Kitchen Hints and Tips to create a small, but full compendium of ways to keep your home life organised, and filled with the most delicious food.

Over three-quarters of a century, Good Housekeeping has built an enviable reputation *for practical, useful advice on running a home, and it is from the pages of Britain's favourite magazine that many of the hints and tips in this book have been gathered. Advice like this doesn't change (a lemon has always soured milk, damp fruit has always sunk to the bottom of a cake mixture), but sadly it can be forgotten. This no longer need be the case. So, seek out your bottle of vinegar to help keep your windows clean, acquire a slotted spoon for skimming fruit stones from your damson jam mixture, and before boiling an egg, don't forget to prick it with a pin to prevent it cracking. Turn the pages and read on for many more such useful snippets.*

CHAPTER ONE

The Storecupboard

*B*e prepared is the good housekeeper's motto, as much as the Scout's, and ever since it first appeared in 1922, Good Housekeeping has extolled the wisdom of maintaining a well-stocked store cupboard. A treasury of all sorts of dry goods, tins, packets and preserved foods saves time and trouble and will allow you to magic up mouthwatering meals when unexpected guests arrive or heavy snow creates siege conditions.

It makes sense to keep stores in daily use in a cupboard in the kitchen, conveniently placed near the worktop, yet as far as possible from any steam and heat. Glass or plastic storage jars with well-fitting lids are the best containers for dry stores, as you can see at a glance how much is in stock. Containers for biscuits and cakes should have tightly fitting lids for maximum freshness.

DRY GOODS

FLOURS, CEREALS AND PULSES, SUGARS, DRIED FRUITS, nuts and seasonings are among the resourceful cook's best allies. Cereals and pulses will keep in good condition for many months. However, since they are susceptible to attack by weevils and mites, and will grow musty and mouldy if allowed to get damp, it is advisable not to store them for indefinite periods.

Common salt

EVEN IF it were not so vital in cookery, no household should be without its supply of salt, for it has an outstanding array of other talents too. Here are just a few listed earlier this century:

In the laundry it prevents the dye in coloured articles from running; it cleanses handkerchiefs; and, mixed with vinegar, it is a good scourer for copper and the sink.

❖

Mixing mustard

Rather than mixing mustard powder with the water as usual, use a little milk instead and also add a pinch of salt. The mustard will retain a stronger colour and not dry up so quickly as when made with water.

TINS AND PACKETS

TINNED FOODS ARE ESSENTIAL ITEMS FOR YOUR store-cupboard as they are excellent standbys and generally last for several years. Packets or boxes of food such as breakfast cereals, jellies and prepared desserts and soups, are vital too, although they cannot be kept as long and must always be stored in a cool, dry place.

Packet jelly

WHEN MAKING up packet jelly try using
ginger ale instead of water, as this long-standing
recipe suggests:

Dissolve the jelly in a small quantity of water, then make up the quantity of liquid with ginger ale. When served with whipped cream, the jelly has just a little pleasing sting in it, but not enough for anyone to guess how it has been made.

DAIRY PRODUCE

EGGS AND CHEESE NEED NOT BE STORED IN THE refrigerator. Instead, as in the past, eggs are best kept in a cool part of the kitchen, while cheese lasts longest in a dish with a ventilated cover. Test eggs for freshness by placing them in a bowl of water: if they sink they are fresh, if they float, they are stale.

To keep cheese

Grate cheese in large quantities at a time and store it in a jar – but not an airtight one, or mould will rapidly develop. Put small pieces of cheese through a mincing machine using the small cutter. It is easier and quicker.

❖

Cracked eggs

TO STOP eggs cracking during boiling, prick them first with a pin or special gadget. If the egg is cracked, it can be boiled without any of the contents leaking out if the following method is adopted:

Add 1 tbsp of salt to the water in which the egg is boiled, rub the crack well with common salt and put the egg at once into the fast-boiling salt water. The white of the egg will not ooze out nor the crack become larger.

Preventing curdling

WHEN BAKING a custard, stand the dish in a tin
of cold water. This will prevent it curdling, as it will
cook more gradually without turning to whey.
If mayonnaise curdles, try the following
rescue measure:

Put another yolk of egg into an empty basin, and add the
curdled sauce gradually to it, stirring all the time.

❖

Making omelettes

USE EITHER a special omelette pan or a good strong
frying pan, and prepare it as described here:

Place it over gentle heat, sprinkle in a little salt and rub the
pan vigorously with crumpled kitchen paper, then dust out
with a dry clean cloth to remove all traces of salt. This is
called seasoning or proving the pan, and helps to prevent
sticking.

Ways with milk

IF YOU want to follow a recipe that requires sour milk and have none available, you can overcome this difficulty by adding a little lemon juice or vinegar to the required quantity of fresh milk.

Put a clean marble in the saucepan when heating milk or a milky substance; it will roll about the pan, and have a similar effect to stirring. Also, if you rinse the pan with water before scalding milk, this will prevent it burning.

HERBS AND SPICES

ALWAYS BUY YOUR SPICES AND HERBS IN SMALL quantities and keep them tightly covered, or they will lose their aroma and flavour. As herbs are used so frequently in cooking, you should store them as near to the cooker as possible.

Bouquet garni

TO MAKE a traditional bouquet garni, tie together thyme, a bayleaf and some parsley, or enclose the herbs in a small muslin bag. For variety, include rosemary, garlic, leek, fennel or sage.

Parsley

THIS IS a culinary plant that is frequently called for in small quantities in the kitchen, and it is not economical to buy much of it at a time because it soon loses its freshness. A simple and oft-used way of having it always to hand is to sow some seeds in an old shallow biscuit tin or any other box that will serve the purpose. It requires no gardening skill to grow it.

Make a few holes in the bottom of the tin and fill it with earth, sprinkle in the seeds and cover lightly with soil. The box may be placed on the back window ledge and it will grow again as often as it is cut. Thyme may also be grown in the same way.

❖

Other advice from the annals of *Good Housekeeping* on the subject of parsley suggests:

Wash parsley in cold water and if it has withered, allow it to stand for an hour or two in the cold water. It should then be well shaken to remove the water, and placed in a glass jar, such as a fruit bottling jar, provided with a cover. If the jar is placed in a refrigerator or in the coolest part of a larder, the parsley keeps perfectly fresh for several days.

*Q*uick Tips

A saucer or linen bag of *powdered charcoal* in the larder will keep food fresh and also absorb smells that arise from certain foods, preventing the odour being taken up by other articles. Milk and butter are renowned for assimilating almost any strong smell, but a dish of charcoal nearby will prevent this.

A little *lemon juice* added to the cooking water will make rice white and fluffier.

When *egg yolks* are left over, if you cover them with cold water in a bowl, they will keep quite fresh until the following day without a skin forming.

If you use a wet knife to slice *hard-boiled eggs* they will not disintegrate so readily.

Walnuts shell more easily if warmed first.

Pasta is less likely to boil over when cooking if you add a tablespoon of olive oil to the water.

CHAPTER TWO

Baking

Cake making is a big subject, and one in which the traditionally-minded homemaker has always striven to shine. But it is not nearly as complicated as it appears at first sight to the novice, for although there are many different cakes, the methods of making them are, in fact, few. Cakes are classified as plain, rich or sponge, according to the proportion of fat, sugar and eggs they contain and the method by which they are made. Gingerbreads form a small – but sensational – subsidiary to plain cakes. When baking, it is not necessary to learn a great many recipes, but rather to try to master the method of making and baking each type of cake. Then you will be able to attempt any cake recipe you come across, confident of success.

CAKE MAKING

WHEN IT comes to first principles, the advice below, even though it was dispensed in the pages of *Good Housekeeping* several decades ago, still holds true today.

◆ To make a good cake, it is wise to assemble all the necessary equipment before beginning the actual measuring or mixing. Place all the ingredients on the work surface and allow them to come to room temperature.

◆ Read the cake recipe all the way through. Follow the recipe exactly making no substitutions of ingredients, no changes in amounts and no changes in directions. Never double or halve a cake recipe; this usually means trouble. It takes a little longer, but you will be sure of the results, if you make up the exact recipe as many times as needed.

◆ Also use the exact ingredients called for, such as double-acting baking powder and cake flour. This can mean the difference between a masterpiece and a mediocrity. Bake the cake at the temperature and for the time period specified.

◆ Use pans that are the exact size and depth indicated. Bigger, smaller, or shallower pans than those called for can cause a cake to fail.

◆ Be sure metal cake pans are bright and shiny inside and out, so cakes will brown evenly and delicately. Dull, dark pans cause cakes to brown too fast, too unevenly. To keep cake pans shiny, clean them with steel-wool soap pads.

Choosing the type of cake

CAKES CAN be grouped into three main classes – plain, rich and sponge – according to the method of making them and the proportion of fat, sugar and eggs which they contain. These defining characteristics are outlined here:

Plain cake mixtures contain up to half fat and sugar to flour, and the fat is rubbed into the flour, the so-called rubbing-in method.

Rich cake mixtures contain higher proportions of fat and sugar. This necessitates a different method of making; the fat and sugar are creamed together, the egg beaten in and the flour folded into the mixture: the creaming method.

Sponge cake mixtures usually contain no fat, but a high proportion of eggs and sugar. The eggs and sugar are whisked together and the flour folded in very lightly, this being known as the whisking method.

Greasing cake tins

USE UNSALTED or clarified fat when preparing the
cake tins and make sure that you have done this
before you begin to make the cake mixture.

The quickest method is to brush over the tin with a pastry
brush dipped in the melted fat. For sponge cakes, grease the
tin, then dust with 1 tsp flour mixed with 1 tsp caster sugar.

❖

Lining cake tins

FOR RICH mixtures and fruit cakes, line the whole tin;
for sponge sandwiches, line the bottom of the tin only.
Greaseproof paper will provide the best results, and
should be greased carefully. The conscientious cook
would do this by following these instructions:

Cut a piece of paper long enough to go around the tin and
high enough to stand about 5 cm (2 in) above the top edge;
cut another piece to fit the bottom. Fold up the bottom edge
of the long strip about 3 cm (1¼ in) and snip with scissors.
The band will then fit a square, round or oval tin neatly.
Brush both pieces with melted fat. Place the strips in
position first; the bottom piece will then keep the snipped
edge of the band in position and make a neat lining.

For a rectangular tin, cut the paper about 5 cm (2 in) larger all around than the tin. Place the tin on it and make a cut to each corner of the tin. Grease both paper and tin and fit in the paper, overlapping it at the corners.

❖

Cake ingredients

'ALWAYS USE the best ingredients possible when making a cake and be sure to use the kind of shortening called for in the recipe. Whatever the shortening, in cakes made by the conventional method, it should be beaten with the sugar until light and fluffy, almost like whipped cream. In one-bowl method cakes, add the shortening, plus part or all of the liquid, directly to the sifted dry ingredients before beating,' wrote *Good Housekeeping's* cookery editor in 1958 – fundamentals don't change. She then continued:

Flour Self-raising flour may be used for plain cakes, but for richer cakes and sponges it is better to use plain flour plus a suitable quantity of a reliable raising agent.

When measuring sifted flour, spoon it lightly into the measuring cup, scraping the top level with a spatula or straight-edged knife. Then resift again with baking powder and salt, or as recipe directs.

Eggs Always use fresh eggs and, if the recipe calls for them to be separated, then separate them over small bowls before transferring to a larger bowl for mixing – the merest hint of yolk in the white will prevent it from thickening.

Raising agents Use a reliable brand of baking powder and measure accurately. Bicarbonate of soda combined with cream of tartar is sometimes used, especially for scones. Whisked or creamed mixtures, as long as they contain the correct proportion of eggs, need very little extra raising agent. Bicarbonate of soda only acts as a raising agent when mixed with cream of tartar and moistened – it is then that carbon dioxide is formed.

Fats Butter is the ideal fat to use; its flavour is good and the cakes keep well. Margarine is a good substitute, and lard and white vegetable fats can be used in conjunction with margarine or butter. Dripping, which can be used for some fruit cakes, should be mild in flavour and well clarified.

Sugar Granulated sugar is satisfactory for plain cakes, but caster sugar is better for creamed mixtures and sponges. Demerara is often used for gingerbreads.

To measure granulated sugar, spoon it lightly into the measuring cup and level it off with a spatula or straight-edge knife. To measure brown sugar, pack it firmly into the cup using the back of a spoon. When turned out it should hold the shape of the cup.

Stale cake crumbs These are ideal for making gingerbread and cheesecakes. Any favourite recipe can be taken, but the proportion of crumbs depends on their quality; for example, those from sponge cakes, which contain no fat, can be regarded as flour and used in the same way, except that twice as many crumbs as flour are required. When using crumbs from rich mixtures such as Genoese sponge or Madeira, a smaller proportion of butter and sugar than given in the ingredients would be necessary as the crumbs already contain a fairly large proportion of these two commodities.

❖

Creating the mixture

BE VERY careful not to overbeat or underbeat cake
batter: beat it for only the time specified or to the
described state. Either underbeating or overbeating
batter can cause cake failure.

When folding in dry ingredients, use a large metal spoon, running it along the bottom of the bowl and up again in one smooth action. Then cut down through the bowl, rotating the bowl as you fold.

Baking a cake

THE BAKING of a consummate cake has always been a highly-regarded skill, to be acquired and honed to perfection over years of practice. In early issues of *Good Housekeeping*, advice such as this was proffered to novice cake-makers:

Just before starting to mix your cake, start heating the oven so it will be at the indicated temperature when the cake is ready to be baked. Then, when the minimum baking time is up, peek in the oven and lightly touch the centre of the cake. If the cake springs back and no imprint remains, it is done. For a double check, insert a cake tester or toothpick – it must be clean when you remove it for the cake to be done.

Make it a practice to have your oven temperature control checked periodically. Too slow an oven may cause the cake to rise and then fall, producing a heavy, coarse cake. Too hot an oven may cause the cake surface to break and have a cracked appearance and usually a hump, too.

To make the cake still better

The temperature of the oven and the length of time the cake is cooked for are not the only things that need concern the cook. Fine attention to detail improves the recipes still further.

When pouring batter into lightly greased and floured pans, or into pans lined with waxed paper, spread it evenly with a rubber spatula, beginning in the centre and spreading to the edge of the pan. If you are making a sponge-type cake, cut through the batter several times to remove the air bubbles. If making separate layers, divide the batter evenly (a scale, if you have one, is ideal for this purpose) so the layers will be uniform.

When placing the pans in the preheated oven, make sure they do not touch; air must circulate around each pan. Cakes may be baked on both oven racks at the same time, if they are placed diagonally. Opening the oven door prior to minimum baking time is unwise because it may cause a cake to fail.

After removing a butter-type cake from the oven, let it stand in the pan on a wire cake rack for about 10 minutes so the cake will leave the sides of the pan freely and will be less likely to break. Then carefully remove the cake from the pan and finish cooling on the rack.

After removing a sponge-type cake from the oven, invert the pan and let the cake hang in the pan until it is cold. Now insert a spatula directly against the pan, then pull it out. Repeat around the edges and the tube. Then invert the cake on the rack and lift off the pan. For high, fluffy wedges in sponge-type cakes, pull the pieces apart with two forks.

CAKE-MAKING FAULTS

OVER THE YEARS A RICH ARCHIVE OF INFORMATION about cake-making problems has been gathered together at the *Good Housekeeping* offices. Here are the most frequently-raised readers' problems, with words of advice to rectify the problems.

Most cake troubles can be traced to:

◆ not using the ingredients called for. Substitutes are not the same, even though they may look so.

◆ not using accurate, level measurements. Small variations in amounts of ingredients may affect volume, texture, or crust.

◆ not baking in the right pan, at the right temperature, for the right time.

If your cake sinks in the middle:

◆ the cake is not cooked through. Check up on the baking time and temperature, and be sure that the cake responds to the test before removing it from the oven.

◆ there has been a sudden drop in the oven temperature at a critical stage of the cooking. Avoid opening the oven door too often or too suddenly, and do not alter the position of the cake while it is still soft. See that no draught blows directly onto the oven from the kitchen door or window.

◆ there is too much raising agent, causing the mixture to 'over-work' itself.

◆ the mixture is too wet. Test the consistency carefully before putting it in the tin.

◆ there is too much sugar in proportion to the other ingredients.

❖

If the fruit sinks to the bottom of your cake:

◆ the mixture is too slack to support the fruit.

◆ the fruit is not properly dried after washing.

◆ the oven temperature is too low.

◆ the fruit is in too large pieces.

If your cake is heavy and sticky inside:

◆ it has been baked at too high a temperature and for too short a time, so that the outside has cooked too quickly, leaving the centre slightly raw. Reduce the heat next time you use the recipe or place the cake lower in the oven. Be sure to allow the full baking time.

◆ the mixture has been made too wet, so that the cake does not dry out in the centre.

◆ the cake has cooled too suddenly. See that the cake is not put in a draughty place when first taken from the oven.

◆ the cake has been packed away while still warm. Make sure the cake is absolutely cold before putting it away in the cake tin.

❖

If your cake suffers from a close or heavy texture:

◆ there is not enough raising agent. Check on the recipe, and measure the baking power accurately. If the cake is raised by air beaten into the mixture, perhaps you are not beating sufficiently thoroughly.

◆ heavy handling has occurred. Cakes require a very light touch, especially when mixing in the dry ingredients.

◆ the mixture is too dry. If it is not moistened enough, the cake is likely to be close and dry when baked.

◆ the mixture is too wet. Too much liquid when mixing causes the cake to have a close, heavy texture.

If your cake tasted dry, it was probably left too long in the oven, or perhaps the oven was too slow. Both overcooking and baking at too low a temperature will cause a cake to dry unduly.

If the texture is coarse and open, you have probably used too much raising agent.

A cake that boils out through a crack in the top was put into too hot an oven. If the initial temperature is too high, the outside of the cake sets and forms a crust before the cake starts to cook in the centre; then, instead of rising evenly, the mixture has to force its way out of the top.

CAKE DECORATING

IN 1961, *The Good Housekeeping Book of Cake Decorating* was published. Many of its tried-and-tested hints still hold true today and would be best attended to by any would-be cake decorator.

Making uncooked icings

ONE IMPORTANT point to remember is that icing is always at its best on the day it goes on the cake, although many icings may stay fresh for several days. Never start to make the icing until you have read the recipe from beginning to the end and do be careful about measurements.

A good uncooked icing has a trio of virtues: a fine flavour; creamy, glossy texture; and an uncracked appearance when cut. To help achieve these, make sure the fat is at room temperature. Butter may be substituted for part of the shortening if a butter flavour is desired, but the icing will not be as white as when shortening only is used, and it will be a little softer.

If mixing ingredients in an electric mixer, use a low speed to avoid whipping air into the icing: it should not be aerated at all; rather, it should be very smooth.

When the icing is mixed, put it in a container that can be tightly closed. If air is kept from the icing it will remain smooth. Store the container in a cool place but do not refrigerate unless your kitchen is quite hot, and then the icing will always be ready to use.

After removing some of the icing from the container, but sure to re-cover the container at once so the icing will remain smooth.

❖

Making cooked icings

A GOOD cooked icing is distinguishable by its uncracked, glossy exterior; soft, delicate texture; well-blended flavour and fluffy exterior. Cook the icing exactly as the recipe directs; for example, if it says 'cook over boiling water', be sure the water really is boiling.

Be sure that the beater and bowls are free from grease.

Have egg whites at room temperature before using. This makes for greater volume.

Separate the whites from the yolks carefully so that not even a speck of yoke is in the whites.

A cooked icing should be cooled slightly before using, or it will soak into the cake.

Colouring icing

LIQUID FOOD colour can be bought in bottles
or plastic tubes, but it is not necessary to buy every
colour of the rainbow. If you keep the four basic
colours – red, yellow, blue and green – in your
storecupboard, you can use them to make a palette of
other striking colours. For example, mix together:

Orange: 3 drops red and 5 drops yellow

Violet: 1 drop red and 2 drops blue

Brown: 4 drops yellow, 1 drop green, 3 drops red

Peach: 2 drops red and 5 drops yellow

Lime: 3 drops yellow and 1 drop green

Strawberry: 5 drops red and 3 drops yellow.

For additional colour blends, check the package labels, or
experiment yourself.

When working with food colouring it is always advisable to
use a relatively small amount, for a little goes a long way. To
add liquid food colour to white frosting, shake or add it with
a toothpick, a few drops at a time. Generally speaking, it is
easier to duplicate the colours found in nature than to
reproduce such colours as black or grey.

PASTRY MAKING

PASTRY MAKING CAN DAUNT EVEN AN OTHERWISE confident cook as much as a complete beginner. Yet it need hold no terrors for the *Good Housekeeping* reader. In every decade, the magazine has drawn on its expertise and experience to guide each new generation step by step through the basic pastry types and principles, simplifying seemingly complex techniques so as to ensure success. And once you have the key elements off pat, you will be able to tackle the most adventurous of recipes. *Good Housekeeping's* counsel in 1953 still cannot be bettered.

'She has a wonderfully light hand with pastry.' This tribute is coveted by every cook – and often in vain. Yet pastry making is not a difficult art; the secret of success lies primarily in coolness at every stage of the preparation, as little handling as possible, and a really hot oven. Watch these points, follow a reliable recipe, and your pastry will be light, crisp and delicious.

As a general rule, plain flour is recommended. Self-raising flour gives good results with the plainer pastries, but the texture is slightly different. Heat the oven to the correct temperature before putting in the pastry – the richer the mixture, the higher the temperature. When making pies with raw meat, poultry or vegetable fillings, lower the heat when the crust is cooked, covering it with a double thickness of greaseproof paper to prevent it becoming too brown.

Choosing the type of pastry

THERE ARE seven main types of pastry – shortcrust (both plain and flan), sweetcrust, flaky, puff, rough puff, hot-water crust and choux. The chief difference between them is the method of introducing the fat. In the short pastries, it is rubbed into the flour; in suetcrust, the chopped suet is simply mixed in, without further manipulation; in the puff and flaky types, the fat is rolled into the dough; in hot-water crust and choux pastry, the fat is melted in hot liquid before being added to the flour.

❖

Flaky pastry

THIS IS formed of thin, crisp layers. It is similar to puff pastry and is cooked at the same temperature, but it is not as light and has fewer layers. It is made by folding and rolling dough into layers and daubing fat in between. The pieces of fat cause air pockets to form, and then help to separate the flakes.

Shortcrust pastry

IN THIS simplest and most widely used pastry, the fat is rubbed into the flour with the fingertips; it is important to carry out this operation very quickly and lightly, raising the hands high while working to incorporate as much cold air as possible. Add only enough water to bind the dry ingredients into a ball – too much water makes a sticky, difficult-to-handle mixture, resulting in a tough pastry. The mixture should bind together into one lump, leaving the sides of the bowl clean. In warm weather, one or two cubes of ice, placed in the water used for mixing, will help to keep the dough cool.

❖

Rough puff pastry

THIS IS more quickly made than either flaky or true puff, so it is a favourite with the busy cook.

Hot-water crust pastry

TRADITIONALLY ENGLISH, this economical pastry is used for meat pies that are to be eaten cold. Unlike most pastries, it is mixed with hot water and milk, so that it can be easily moulded into shape to make 'raised' pies. For smaller and simpler shapes it is possible to mould the pastry by hand, but if a more elaborately decorated shape is required it is necessary to use a special pie mould, which opens at the side so that it can be removed when the pie is cooked.

❖

Suetcrust pastry

THIS IS used for a number of substantial puddings, both savoury and sweet; it is more often steamed or boiled than baked, since this tends to make it hard.

❖

Choux pastry

THE CHARACTERISTIC light, airy texture of this pastry makes it suitable for dainty sweet or savoury confections such as eclairs filled with cream, custard or a savoury mixture; and for cream buns and profiteroles.

To Make Perfect Pastry

As with cake making, practice makes perfect for the aspiring pastry cook. The more recipes you try, the more you will come to understand the reasons behind the rules and develop an enviably professional expertise.

Coolness is the key to good results. Handle the pastry as little as possible and always use the fingertips for rubbing in the fat. Rich pastries are improved by being cooled on a cold slab or in the refrigerator between rollings.

Always sieve the flour and salt together into the mixing bowl, as this helps to lighten the mixture. Additional air may be incorporated by lifting the flour from the bowl with the fingertips when rubbing in.

The liquid should be very cold and must be added carefully; an excess causes a sticky, unmanageable dough, and any extra flour then added will alter the proportions of the ingredients and cause the pastry to be tough.

For extra-light pastry, add a little lemon juice to the water when mixing.

When the term 'knead' is used, the technique must be less vigorous than for bread dough, and very brief. Pastry dough is kneaded by using a combination of rolling, pressing and patting, not by pounding with the knuckles.

Rolling out must be done lightly and firmly; do not roll more than necessary.

Work quickly when preparing, rolling, shaping and filling pastry. If pastry is uncovered for a long time during its preparation, it tends to dry on the surface.

To make pastry easier to handle and 'shorter' when cooked, and to prevent shrinkage during cooking, leave it to 'rest' before rolling it out. Cover it and put it in the refrigerator for about 20 minutes.

Avoid stretching pastry when rolling out, as this will result in shrinkage during baking.

To get the optimum rise from flaky pastries, bake on a damp baking sheet.

Baking blind is done to bake a pie shell or flan case partially or fully before filling it with a mixture which would otherwise make the bottom soggy, or with fruit that does not need to be cooked. Weight the pastry with dried beans, rice or pasta to prevent it rising during baking.

Brown glaze pastry by adding a pinch of salt to the beaten egg.

Pastry requires a hot oven. Too slow an oven causes pale, hard pastry.

YEAST COOKERY

WHAT COULD BE MORE TRADITIONAL AND NOURISHING than home-made bread? The aroma alone is enough to set tastebuds tingling. Home-made buns, bread and yeast cakes are so delicious that even if they are only made occasionally, they will invariably be the focus of attention at the family tea-table. Use either baker's yeast, bought fresh as required, or failing this, tinned dried yeast, which should be used according to the manufacturer's directions.

The function of yeast is to act as a raising agent, creating bubbles of gas which will lift the dough and make it light and spongy in texture. The yeast must be kept at a warm, even temperature throughout the bread or bun making.

❖

Yeast and heat

Excess heat will destroy yeast, so avoid it until the mixture is put into the oven, by which time the yeast will have completed its magical task.

Ensure that all liquids used are at blood heat and that the dough is put to rise in a warm (not hot) place, covered with a cloth to keep out draughts, which would delay the process.

*Q*uick Tips

To soften hard *butter*, cut it into small pieces, boil a few tablespoons of milk and pour it on to the butter. Mash all together then pour away any surplus liquid. By this method, butter can be softened in two minutes.

When using the *rubbing in* method, grate hard butter straight from the refrigerator into the flour mixture.

Cut *iced cakes* with a knife dipped in boiling water first to prevent cracking the icing.

Cook *rich cakes* at lower temperatures than plainer ones.

To *toast coconut*, spread out desiccated coconut thinly in a shallow pan. Place in a medium-hot oven to toast until delicately browned, stirring the coconut or shaking the pan often to toast it evenly.

Freshen a *stale loaf* by sprinkling it with water, putting it in a cloth dipped in water and then well wrung out, and placing it in a hot oven for 10 minutes. When you remove it from the oven, take off the cloth and replace the loaf in the oven for a further 5 minutes: it will look and taste like new bread.

Cake will remain moist if you include a slice of bread or an apple in the tin. Biscuits stay crisp if some sugar cubes are placed in the tin with them.

CHAPTER THREE

Meat and Poultry

*I*n days gone by, meat was considered the essential core of any good meal: the hallowed meat and two veg was the housewife's sure way to keep her family not just happy but healthy, too. For it was an article of faith that 'meat not only makes the basis of a good, satisfying meal, but it also supplies us with protein, some of the B vitamins and iron; the fat, which is of high energy value, helps to give the meat some of its characteristic flavour.'

The prudent readers of Good Housekeeping *would also have been aware that the price of meat varies according to the type of cut, the most expensive joints being the parts that are least exercised and are therefore usually tender. These cuts can be roasted, fried or grilled, while the tougher parts need slower methods of cooking to soften them. The cheaper cuts are, however, just as nutritious as the dearer ones and have just as good a flavour.*

x

CHOOSING MEAT AND POULTRY

ALWAYS LOOK FOR MEAT WHICH HAS A FIRM AND slightly elastic texture; the lean should be finely grained, the fat firm and free from brown spots or marks; there should not be an excessive amount of fat. The following are some noteworthy points raised by *Good Housekeeping's* cookery editor in 1950 to ensure satisfaction when buying meat.

Beef

The lean of good beef should be a bright red colour, and finely marbled with fat. The solid fat should be pale yellow in colour, and smooth in texture; choose joints with little gristle dividing fat from lean. The most tender meat comes from the upper back, whereas cuts that require longer cooking come from the more heavily muscled areas of the legs and rear.

❖

Lamb

The younger the animal, the paler the flesh; in a young lamb it is light pink, while in a mature animal it is light red. A slight blue tinge to the bones suggests that the animal is young. Imported lamb has a firm white fat, while English lamb has creamy-coloured fat.

Pork

The lean part of pork should be pale pink, moist and slightly marbled with fat. There should be a good outer layer of firm, white fat, with a thin, elastic skin; if the joint is to be roasted, ask the butcher to score the rind. Look for bones that are small and pinkish, which denote a young animal.

❖

Know your bacon slices

Middle-cut or prime bacon is cut from the middle rib area and contains a large eye of lean meat.

Streaky bacon has alternating strips of lean and fat and is cut from the tail end of the loin.

Back bacon is leaner than the other cuts and is cut from the loin.

❖

Chicken

When buying a fresh bird, pinch the tip of the breastbone with your thumb and finger. In a young bird this is soft and flexible; if it is hard and rigid the bird is probably too old to roast satisfactorily and will have to be steamed or boiled. Look at the feet as well – in a young bird they are smooth with small scales and short spurs.

Duck

Choose a young bird with soft, pliable feet; the feet and the bill should be yellow. The name 'duckling' applies to a bird between six weeks and three months old. Ducklings are more commonly eaten than fully grown ducks.

CARVING MEAT

Possessors of this ancient skill, able to cut the meat neatly in the way best suited to the particular joint, have always been highly prized, for expert carving can make a joint go much further. Since meat is usually easier to chew, and so seems most tender, when cut across its grain, the apprentice would study the structure of the joint to be carved, so as to know where the fat and the lean meat are to be found. Leave meat to stand, covered, for 10-20 minutes after cooking and before carving. Place it on a warmed platter (a spiked platter for joints, where it will not slip and where juices than seep out can be saved). Never carve meat or poultry on wooden boards, as there is a great risk of cross-contamination.

The first essential for good carving is a really sharp knife. For carving game and poultry a smaller knife is needed than for a large joint of meat; a long, thin and flexible knife is favoured for carving boned ham, tongue and other pressed, boneless meats. A carving fork should have two sharp, long prongs and a metal guard to protect the carver's hand should the knife slip.

To sharpen a carving knife, draw both sides of the blade in turn smoothly down and across a steel or stone, using rapid strokes, until the blade is sufficiently sharp. This process requires some practice – if it is badly done, the knife may be damaged.

❖

Boneless joints of beef

Carve thinly and across the grain, usually horizontally, with any fat distributed evenly between the slices.

❖

Sirloin or rib of beef (with bone)

Cut the meat from the top of the joint in thin slices downwards from the outside layer of fat to the rib bone, cutting parallel to the bone.

❖

Shoulder of lamb

Place the joint so that the bladebone points away from the carver. Insert the fork securely in the meat, and raise the far side of the joint slightly, then make a vertical cut through the centre of the meat up to the bone; this will cause the joint to open out slightly, making it appear as if a slice has already been removed. Cut thick slices from each side of this gap, as far as the blade bone on the one side and the knuckle on the other; slices of knuckle may also be carved for those who appreciate it. Next, turn the joint so that the bladebone faces the carver, and carve the meat on top of the bladebone downwards in strips, parallel with the central fin of the bone. Finally, turn the joint upside down and carve the meat from the underside horizontally in slices.

❖

Leg of lamb

Slice the meat downwards in thick slices from the surface to the bone, starting at the thick end. Work towards the end of the leg, slicing at a slight angle.

❖

Loin of lamb or pork

Cut the joint right through, downwards, into chops. This is easier if the bone has been chined.

❖

Best end of neck of lamb

Cut the joint right through, downwards into cutlets.

Saddle of lamb

First carve the meat from the top of the joint in long slices, cutting downwards and parallel with the backbone. Do this on each side and then turn the joint upside down and slice the meat from the underside in a similar manner.

❖

Leg of pork

Use the point of the knife to cut through the crackling, and include some with each serving; if necessary, lift it off and cut it on the dish. Cut the meat as for leg of lamb, but in slices of medium thickness.

❖

Stuffed breast of lamb

Cut downwards in fairly thick slices, right through the joint.

❖

Chicken and turkey

Use a sharp knife with a short, stiff blade or a kitchen knife – either of these are easier to use than an ordinary meat carver. Remove the wings first, gently easing them away from the body, and cut through the joint gristle. Next, remove the legs, prising the leg outwards with the fork and cutting through the joint. You can then cut the breast into thin slices, parallel with the breastbone.

ACCOMPANIMENTS

The following list prescribes the time-honoured correct accompaniments to serve with meat, poultry and game. Gravy made from the juices in the baking tin should also be served with a roast.

Roast beef Yorkshire pudding, horseradish sauce.

Roast lamb Mint sauce.

Roast mutton Caper or onion sauce.

Roast pork Apple sauce, sage and onion stuffing.

Roast turkey Chestnut or sausage forcemeat, bread sauce, bacon rolls, sausages.

Roast chicken Bread sauce, sausages, bacon rolls, forcemeat stuffing.

Roast duck or goose Sage and onion stuffing, apple sauce.

Roast wild duck, widgeon and teal Orange salad, orange sauce.

Roast pheasant, partridge, grouse Bread sauce, fried crumbs, chipped potatoes, green salad (lettuce or watercress).

Bacon rolls

THESE ARE the perfect accompaniment for roast turkey
or chicken and are encouragingly easy to make.

Use thin-cut rashers and remove the rind. Stretch the
rashers by stroking along the length with a heavy knife.
Either roll up the whole rasher or cut each in half crosswise
before rolling.

❖

Mint sauce

MAKE THIS accompaniment at least 1 hour before
serving with roast lamb.

Put mint leaves with 2 tsp of sugar on a board and chop
finely. Tip into the server, add 1 tbsp of boiling water and
stir until the sugar has dissolved. Stir in vinegar to taste (1-
2 tbsp).

❖

Apple sauce

SERVED WITH pork or sausages, apple sauce perfectly
complements the texture and taste of the meat.

Slice the apples and boil gently in an open saucepan with 2-
3 tbsp water until soft and thick. Then beat to a pulp with a
wooden spoon and, to finish, stir in 25 g (1 oz) butter and a
little sugar if the apples are very tart.

Q*uick Tips*

Coat pieces of meat with flour by putting them in a paper bag with the flour then shaking well. The same principle applies to breadcrumbs.

If you snip the fat on thick slices of *bacon* after removing the rind it prevents the bacon curling up during cooking.

If you are using a *meat thermometer* in a roast joint, insert it in the thickest part of the meat, away from the fat or bone, before this is put into the oven.

Beef stock should be made from the finest fresh ingredients. It will keep for a week in a refrigerator and for up to four months if frozen. If you are freezing stock for use in small quantities, freeze it in an ice-cube tray, remove when frozen and place the cubes in a labelled and dated plastic bag.

If meat is *cooked on a rack* or grid standing inside a roasting tin, the finished result will be less fatty.

If the *hot fat and juices* from the tin are spooned over the joint several times during the cooking period, the flavour is improved and the meat is moist and juicy.

Sprinkling roast meat with flour and salt 15 minutes before the cooking is finished results in a *crisp outside*.

CHAPTER FOUR

Fish

The traditional way of grouping fish has always been into saltwater and freshwater types. Another classification, which cuts across these two groups, is into white and oily fish. White fish have a low fat content and characteristic white flesh; familiar examples are cod, haddock, hake, sole, plaice and turbot. Oily fish have a high fat content and their flesh is usually darker; the best known are herring, mackerel, eel and salmon. Shellfish constitute a separate group. Fish is an excellent source of protein and oily fish also supply beneficial fats plus vitamins A and D.

BUYING AND CLEANING FISH

DESPITE THE ADVENT OF THE DEEP FREEZE, COOKS seeking optimum flavour and texture will always choose fresh over frozen fish. In the guidelines *Good Housekeeping* gave its readers in 1953, it advised cooking fish as soon as possible after buying. It also suggested looking for fish that is in season – some kinds can be bought all the year round, while others have a closed season (usually covering the spawning period). Nowadays, every cook can demand that the fish bought from the fishmonger's slab should display all the signs of complete freshness – firm flesh, bright eyes, red gills, with the characteristic skin markings clear and bright.

Never be tempted to purchase fish that does not satisfy you on these points, for not even the most skilled hand can put back the flavour into the 'not-so-fresh'. Go marketing with an open mind, so that you can select the fish that is the day's best 'buy'.

To clean white fish

IF YOU buy fresh fish whole you may always ask your fishmonger to clean and skin it for you. However, if necessary, the traditional cook took pride in being able to perform this task:

Scrape off any scales, working from the tail towards the head. Slit the fish and remove and discard the entrails, retaining only the roe if this is in good fat condition. Rub with kitchen salt to remove any black skin. Remove fins and gills, and the head, if required. Rinse the fish in cold water.

❖

To skin and fillet fish

LIKEWISE, SKINNING and filleting are useful skills to have at your fingertips.

With flat fish, the dark skin is usually removed, whatever the method of cooking; white skin is usually left on unless the fish is very large. Prepare and clean the fish as above, then make a slit across the skin close to the tail and loosen it sufficiently to get a good grip on it. Dip the fingers in salt, then, holding the fish down firmly with the other hand, draw the skin off towards the head.

Filleted fish may be skinned in the same way. However, round fish skin less easily. Work from the head towards the tail, taking great care not to tear the fish.

Four fillets can be obtained from flat fish, two from each side. Use a sharp, pliable knife and make an incision down the backbone, cutting to the bone. Using the point of the knife, work from the centre cut towards the outside and from head to tail, and with long strokes, remove the flesh close to the bone. When two fillets have been removed, turn the fish over and remove the other two. When you have finished, the bones should be quite clean and may be used with any skin for making fish stock for sauce if required.

CARVING FISH

THE AIM IN CARVING FISH IS TO SERVE IT IN NEAT portions without breaking up the flakes or mixing them with the bones or skin. A keen-edged blade is not necessary – in fact, a blunt edge is preferable.

Cod

Lay the fish flat on a dish on its side. First run the knife from head to tail through the middle of the flesh on the side uppermost, taking the knife down as far as the backbone, but not through it. Then cut slices of the flesh from each side of this centre cut, slicing at right angles to it. When all the fish is served, removed the backbone and cut the lower half as before.

Sole and plaice

Cut right through the bone into sections across the fish. First cut off the head, then cut through, widthways, into two, three or even four portions.

❖

Turbot

Lay the fish flat on a dish. First cut through the flesh down the middle of the fish up to the bone but not through it. Then cut fairly wide slices from each side of the centre cut, at right angles to the centre. When all the fish is served from the upperside, remove the backbone and then serve the underside, cutting it in a similar fashion.

❖

Salmon

Lay the fish flat on a dish on its side. First cut right through the middle of the flesh from top to bottom, cutting up to, but not through, the bone. Carve the thick part of the fish in slices lengthwise (the back), making the cuts parallel to the first cut. With each serving, include a slice of the thin part of the fish (the belly), cutting the slices widthways from this part.

SHELLFISH

THE UNVARYING ADVICE WHEN BUYING SHELLFISH IS only to buy when in season, and to eat them when they are as fresh as possible. Here are some notes from the *Good Housekeeping Cookery Book*, first published in 1948, on their choice and use:

Clams

In season all year round, but best in autumn. Sold live in its shell. Usually eaten raw like oysters. Otherwise cook as for mussels. Also available canned and smoked.

Cockles

Available all year round, but best from September to April. Usually sold cooked and shelled. Can be used in dishes in place of mussels or oysters, or eaten plain with vinegar.

Crab

At its best from May to August. Can also be bought canned and frozen. Crabs are usually sold ready boiled and many fishmongers will also prepare and dress them. The edible portion of the crab consists of two parts – the white flesh of the claws and legs, and the 'brown' meat, usually mixed with breadcrumbs for smooth consistency.

❖

Crawfish

Often called the spiny lobster, it resembles a lobster without the big claws, and is prepared and cooked like a lobster. Also obtainable canned and frozen.

❖

Lobster

In season all the year round, but at its best in the summer months; lobster is sometimes difficult to obtain from December to April. Like crabs, lobsters are usually sold ready boiled. Lobster meat may also be bought ready prepared in cans or frozen whole.

❖

Mussels

In season from September to March. It is not advisable to collect mussels from around the tide lines. They must be alive when bought – discard any with gaping shells, scrub thoroughly and remove byssus threads before cooking. Wash in several changes of water. The last water should be absolutely clean.

❖

Oysters

In season from September to April. When oysters are bought, the shells should be firmly closed. Oysters can be served raw 'on the shell' or cooked in various ways – in patties, as oysters *au gratin*, or added to steak and kidney pudding. Oysters usually live in the mouth of a river or in a bay near the shore, cultivated ones being reared in special beds. When you buy oysters, they should come from a reliable source, for if they are not absolutely fresh they may cause poisoning.

❖

Prawns

Obtainable all the year round, but at their best from February to October. Also sold canned, bottled and frozen. Fresh prawns are usually sold boiled in the shell. Frozen prawns come from different areas around the world. Choose those that come from cold water fishing grounds for cocktails and salads.

Scallops

In season from October to March but at their best in January and February. These can be bought either cleaned and opened, or alive and tightly closed. If open, choose good-sized, white-fleshed scallops, with a bright orange roe. If closed, insert a strong small knife between the shells, forcing them apart; take out the scallops, and discard the black part and the frilly membrane known as the beard. Wash the scallops very thoroughly in cold water, then dry and use as required. They are often served in the deep shell.

❖

Shrimps

Fresh shrimps, pink or brown, are available nearly all the year round; they may also be bought frozen, or potted in butter. The fresh ones are usually sold ready boiled. Shrimps may be served in the same ways as prawns, but, being cheaper, they are also used in fish sauces, chowders and casseroles. Potted shrimps are often served as a 'starter' and should ideally be warmed before serving to melt the butter and bring out the full flavour of shrimps and spices.

Q*uick Tips*

The *smell of fish* is particularly hard to remove from cooking utensils. Wash them as soon as possible after use in lukewarm water to which 2 tbsp of salt or 1 tsp of mustard have been added. If they are then rinsed well in clean water and dried, no smell should linger. Add 1 tsp of vinegar to the washing-up water to eradicate a fish smell from china.

The *liquor* that fish has been steamed in makes a good base for a sauce.

When *grilling fish* whole, make three or four diagonal cuts in the body on each side to allow the heat to penetrate easily.

Serve *lobsters* hot, grilled or in such classic dishes as Lobster Newburg or Thermidor.

Serve *lobster* leftovers in a curry, scalloped, in the form of patties or in omelettes.

Scallops are delicious fried with bacon or served in a cheese sauce.

CHAPTER FIVE

Fruit and Vegetables

*O*ver the decades, Good Housekeeping *has produced a veritable cornucopia of traditional hints and tips for pickling, preserving and cooking fruit and vegetables. Those specially selected for these pages are the most helpful and enduring. It is remarkable to think that some of them first appeared in the magazine some sixty years ago.*

WAYS WITH FRUIT

Apples

TO ENHANCE an apple tart, try sprinkling 2-3 tbsp of orange juice over the apples. This imparts a tangy flavour and gives extra zest to any apples that are inclined to be dry and tasteless.

To prevent peeled apples and pears from discolouring, put the prepared fruit at once into cold water (adding a little lemon juice if you wish), directly into lemon juice or into sugar syrup.

❖

Apricots

The kernels of apricots have an attractive almond flavour, so include a few in apricot preserves.

❖

Bananas

As with apples and pears, a little lemon juice added to sliced bananas immediately after cutting prevents discoloration. Remember, too, that generally the smaller the variety of banana, the sweeter the flesh.

Berries

IF BERRIES are washed the best way, rather than what may seem easiest, there is a great difference in their appearance and taste.

Always put the berries into water, never turn water upon them, for it bruises them, spoils their shape and wastes their juices. Gently and carefully stir the berries about in the water with your fingertips, until all the dust and insects have been dislodged, then lift the berries out on to a square of absorbent cloth, spread in the sun if possible. In 10 minutes, the berries will be dry and ready to hull, looking fresh and beautiful and with all their natural flavour intact.

Grapes

TO PEEL a grape, remove the skin with a sharp knife, or your finger nail. If the skin is obstinate, plunge the grapes into hot water for a second or two, then into cold. Make a small slit in the side of each grape and remove the pips with a fine skewer or leave the grapes whole and use the rounded end of a new hair grip, pushed into the stem end. Whole unskinned grapes can be cut in half and the pips then removed.

Lemons

TO EXTRACT just a small amount of juice from a
lemon, you need only puncture the skin with a fork and
squeeze gently. To obtain as much juice as possible from
a lemon, heat it before cutting and squeezing. Lemon
juice is an excellent source of pectin and so is used
widely in jam making.

❖

Oranges

WHEN MAKING a fruit compote or salad, try soaking
the unpeeled oranges first in boiling water, letting them
stand for five minutes You will find that the white pithy
part will come off quite easily with the skin, leaving the
orange flesh clean for slicing. For a fragrant cup of tea,
add dried tangerine peel to the pot.

Quinces

TO MAKE quince marmalade, wash and brush the quinces and remove the blossom ends. Then cut them in pieces, removing the seeds, and put them into a preserving pan with cold water to cover. Allow the fruit to simmer slowly until reduced to a pulp, then rub through a sieve. Weigh the purée, and to each pound allow ¼ lb sugar. Cook these together for 20 minutes, or until the marmalade will set, stirring frequently to prevent burning. Pour into warm pots and cover when cold.

❖

Rhubarb

THOUGH STRICTLY the stem of a plant, this is usually classed as a fruit. Never eat the leaves of rhubarb as they are poisonous. Chopped, preserved stem ginger is traditionally served with the cooked fruit, perfectly complementing its sharp flavour. You can reduce the acidity of rhubarb by cooking it in cold tea.

VEGETABLE MATTERS

STORE VEGETABLES IN A COOL, AIRY PLACE – FOR example, in a vegetable rack placed in a cool larder or in the vegetable compartment of the refrigerator.

Artichokes

TO PREVENT Jerusalem artichokes discolouring, use a stainless steel knife or peeler to peel them quickly and plunge them immediately into cold water, keeping them under the water as long as possible. A squeeze of lemon juice, or a few drops of vinegar, added to the water helps to keep them a good colour. Globe artichokes should be a good green colour, with tightly clinging, fleshy leaves – purplish centres or leaves that are spreading and fuzzy indicate overmaturity.

❖

Cauliflowers

TO PREVENT the unsightly discoloration of cauliflower, add about half a cupful of milk to the water in which it is to be boiled. Adding 1 tsp of sugar to the cooking water can combat smells from cauliflowers, cabbages and sprouts.

Lettuces

In hot weather, lettuces have a tendency to wilt. This can be prevented by washing the lettuce and leaving it in the water until crisp and firm. If not required immediately, it should then be enclosed in either a clean, wet teacloth or wet paper, which will keep it crisp and fresh. Immersing green vegetables in water for too long causes loss of soluble mineral salts.

❖

Onions

If, after peeling and slicing onions, you rub your hands with a cloth steeped in vinegar, you will remove the onion smell.

To make fried onions more tender, slice them very thinly, put them into a frying pan with a little fat, and cover them with cold water. Boil quickly until the water has evaporated and then fry until brown.

❖

Potatoes

If you grease potato skins before baking, you will improve the flavour, keep the skins tender and cut down on cooking time.

Allow potatoes to lie in hot water for 15 minutes before baking. This not only improves the flavour, but reduces the time required for baking by one half. If crisp and brown potatoes are wanted, brush them over with melted butter or fat before putting them in the oven.

❖

Tomatoes

To peel tomatoes easily, drop them into boiling water and leave for a minute or two. Then with the aid of a sharp knife they can be both quickly and thinly peeled.

A good trick for skinning one or two tomatoes is to spear each one on the end of a fork and twist over a gas flame for a few seconds. The skins will crack and peel off willingly.

❖

To ripen fruit or vegetables

Place on a wire cake-stand which is slightly raised from the surface of the table, in a well-lit spot. As the air will circulate around the fruit, you will not need to keep turning them over to ensure even ripening, and there will be no bruises resulting from pressure on a hard, flat surface.

JAM-MAKING

THE RESULT OF ONE OF THE GREAT TRADITIONAL skills of the British housewife, homemade jam has long been a prime attraction of horticultural shows and hotly-contested competitions across the country. The following tried-and-tested tips will make runny or acidic jams a thing of the past – and a winning rosette yours for the taking.

Jam-making equipment

Preserving pan Choose one made from heavy aluminium, stainless steel or tin-lined copper. It should have a fairly thick base or the jam will tend to burn. The pan should also be wide enough across the top to allow for good evaporation of the water, and deep enough to allow the jam to boil rapidly without splashing all over the cooker. Jams made in copper or brass pans will contain less vitamin C than those made in aluminium or stainless steel pans, and must not be left standing in these pans for any length of time. Copper or brass pans must also not be used for pickles or chutneys, as they are too acidic and would react with the metal.

Slotted spoon This is handy for skimming off any stones as they rise to the surface when you are making jam from fruit such as damsons

Funnel A funnel with a wide tube is useful for jar filling.

Sieve Use a nylon sieve rather than metal, as metal might discolour the fruit.

Jam jars You will need a good supply of glass jars, which should be free from cracks, chips or other flaws. Jars holding 450 g or 900 g (1 lb or 2 lb) are the most useful sizes, as covers are sold for these sizes. Wash them well in warm soapy water and rinse thoroughly in clean warm water. Dry off the jars in a cool oven and use while still hot, so that they do not crack when the boiling jam is added.

Pectin and acid content

THE JAM will set only if there is sufficient pectin, acid and sugar present. Some fruits are rich in pectin and acid and give a good set; these include cooking apples, goose-berries, damsons, redcurrants and blackcurrants, some plums, also Seville oranges, lemons and limes. Those giving a medium set include plums, greengages and apricots, loganberries, blackberries and raspberries. Fruits that are of poor setting quality include strawberries, cherries, pears, melon, marrow and rhubarb.

The pectin test

IF YOU are not sure of the setting qualities of the fruit you are using, the following test can be made.

When the fruit has been cooked until soft and before you add the sugar, take 5 ml (1 tsp) juice, as free as possible from seeds and skin, put it in a glass and when cool add 15 ml (1 tbsp) methylated spirit. Shake. Leave for 1 minute; if the mixture forms a jelly-like clot, then the fruit has a good pectin content. If it does not form a single, firm clot, the pectin content is low and some form of extra pectin will be needed.

❖

To rectify pectin problems

FRUITS THAT lack acid and pectin require the addition of a fruit or a fruit juice that is rich in these substances. Lemon juice is widely used for this purpose, since it aids the setting and at the same time often brings out the flavour of the fruit to which it is added.

Allow 30 ml (2 tbsp) lemon juice to 1.8 kg (4 lb) of a fruit with poor setting properties. Alternatively, use an extract of apple or gooseberry or include the whole fruit, making a mixed fruit jam. Yet another method is to use a commercially bottled pectin – follow the manufacturer's instructions.

Homemade pectin extracts

ANY SOUR cooking apples or crab-apples may be used
for this purpose; also apple peelings and cores and
windfalls, or redcurrants and gooseberries.

Take 900 g (2 lb) fruit, wash it and cut it up without peeling
or coring. Cover with 600-900 ml (1-1½ pt) water and stew
gently for about ¾ hour, until well pulped. Strain through a
jelly bag. Do the pectin test to ensure that the extract has a
high pectin content. Allow 150-300 ml (¼-½ pt) of this
extract to 1.8 kg (4 lb) fruit that is low in pectin.

❖

Which sugar?

GRANULATED SUGAR is suitable and the most economical
for jam making, but less scum is formed with lump sugar
and preserving crystals. There is no completely satisfactory substitute for sugar in jam making. If honey or
treacle is used, the flavour is usually distinctly noticeable.
Glucose and glycerine do not have the same sweetening
power as cane sugar. If any of these have to be used, no
more than half the sugar should be replaced.

Setting

Difficulty is sometimes experienced in getting jams of all kinds to set. This is generally due to one of two reasons: either the use of over-ripe fruit (slightly under-ripe fruit is therefore advised for jam) or failure to cook the fruit sufficiently before adding the sugar. There are three traditional ways of testing for a set:

Temperature test This is the most accurate method. Stir the jam, put in a sugar thermometer and when the temperature reaches 105°C (221°F), a set should be obtained. Some fruits may need 1 degree lower or higher than this, so it is a good idea to combine this test with one of the following:

Saucer test Put a very little of the jam on a cold saucer or plate, allow it to cool, then push the finger across the top of the jam, when the surface should wrinkle. (The pan should be removed from the heat during this test or the jam may boil too long.)

Flake test Remove some jam with a wooden spoon, let it cool a little and then allow the jam to drop. If it has been boiled long enough, drops will run together to form flakes which break off sharply.

*Q*uick Tips

If you haven't a *preserving pan,* use a big, thick-based saucepan, remembering that since most saucepans are not as wide across as a preserving pan, you may need to allow a longer simmering and boiling period for the fruit.

If you don't have a *funnel* for filling jam jars, use a jug or large cup.

A *cherry stoner* prevents hands from becoming stained with cherry juice, and saves time too.

Make appealing *jam-jar covers* by cutting circles from fabric remnants and holding them in place with pieces of string or coloured wool.

When potting *strawberry jam,* allow the mixture to cool for about 15 minutes before being potted to prevent the fruit rising in the jars.

Store homemade jams in a cool, dark place.

CHAPTER SIX

Sauces

No good cook regards a sauce as an optional addition to a meal. It is part of the very foundational structure, with its own special purpose to fulfil. It may be used, for instance, to complement the main dish, offsetting, perhaps, a rich meat with its sharp or sweet flavour. Not only can the right sauce make food more mouthwatering; it can also, by its piquant flavour, stimulate appetite and aid digestion. Some sauces, such as good brown sauces, or cheese sauces, add considerably to the nutritional value of a meal, while the coating sauces, particularly, serve as a culinary beauty treatment, making quite ordinary dishes glamorous and popular. Sauces can make or mar a dish, and perfecting them is an art. To be a consummate sauce-maker, above all else you need a sensitive palate and a judicious sense of balance.

SAUCE SECRETS

Although there is an almost infinite variety of sweet and savoury sauces, they can generally be classified according to how they are thickened: roux (liquid thickened with fat and flour); cornflour or arrowroot; or egg. Once you have perfected the technique for each type of sauce, you will be able to experiment and invent your own unique recipes. Many variations can be produced from one basic recipe; for example, cheese, egg, onion, caper, anchovy and parsley sauces can be created from a plain white sauce. For the best results, remember these pieces of advice handed down through the generations:

Sauces must be carefully made to ensure a smooth, glossy result.

They should be tasted before serving, and the flavourings and seasonings adjusted if required.

Use stock whenever possible for making savoury sauces.

For a fish sauce it is often convenient to make a little fish stock from the skin and bones after the fish has been prepared.

To make a white sauce

One of the traditional sauces of the British kitchen, a smooth, creamy white sauce needs to be made with care to prevent lumps occurring. You will need:
butter, flour, milk, salt and pepper.

Melt some butter in a saucepan and stir in an equal quantity of flour to form a roux. Cook for 1-2 minutes, without browning. Add milk a little at a time, stirring well to keep the mixture smooth, until you have the consistency you require. Bring to the boil, stirring all the time. Cook for 2-3 minutes, beating the sauce to make it smooth and glossy. Add seasonings and flavouring as required.

❖

To make a meat glaze

This is the classic method of making a rich stock. A sauce begun in this way will have a supreme flavour and will serve as a base for soups as well as sauces.
You will need: beef bones, chopped carrot, chopped onion, bouquet garni, water, tomato juice, tomato purée.

Put the beef bones into a baking tin in the oven. Allow to cook in a moderately hot oven until nicely brown. Transfer the bones to a large pan; add carrot and onion. Cover with water, add tomato juice and a little tomato purée, and a bouquet garni. Cook slowly until thick.

*Q*uick Tips

To *keep a sauce warm*, stand the saucepan it is in inside another pan of hot water, and cover the sauce with a lid to prevent a skin forming on the top. If the sauce is very thick, a little water may be run over the top.

As the *flavour* depends largely on the liquid chosen, use water only as a last resort. Because it is easier to add more liquid to a sauce that is too thick than to thicken a too-thin one, always keep some liquid back for last-minute adjustments, .

Arrowroot is indispensable as a thickener in sweet and savoury sauces. It thickens at a lower temperature than flour or cornflour so it can be used in delicate sauces that should not be boiled.

When making a *roux sauce*, cook the flour in the fat gently for a few minutes before adding the milk, never letting it burn. Always use a wooden spoon.

For a *sweet white sauce*, add some sugar and cream or evaporated milk at the last minute.

Allow *bread sauce* to stand in a warm place at the side of the stove for 15 minutes before heating to serve.

For a piquant *orange sauce*, add some port wine to the mixture.

CHAPTER SEVEN

Cleaning

'*Cleanliness is the most essential ingredient in the art of cooking: a dirty kitchen being a disgrace to mistress and maid.*' Good Housekeeping *has faithfully upheld Mrs Beeton's dictum, sharing with readers its tried and tested recipes for a dazzlingly clean cook's domain. In the first half of this century a great deal of time was spent in keeping the home spick and span, although most readers of the time would have employed a maid to perform domestic chores. Without the sophisticated gadgets and cleaning materials of today, gleaming results had often to be achieved by good old elbow grease, but nevertheless there were certain remedies and ways of doing things, handed down through generations, that still hold good today.*

To make a home-made polish

THIS TRADITIONAL recipe is quick to make and highly effective. Keep it well out of children's reach, in a bottle that is clearly marked, to prevent accidents:

For a homemade polish, mix together equal quantities of turpentine and linseed with half equal quantities of methylated spirits and vinegar. Shake well before use. This makes a most efficient polish for furniture and all kinds of leather work, papier-mâché, and leather trunks. Apply the mixture sparingly with a soft rag and then polish the furniture with an old silk duster.

To make your own polishing cloth for wood surfaces, put one eggcupful of vinegar and one of paraffin in a screwtop jar. Stuff a clean duster in the jar, screw on the lid and leave overnight. The duster will absorb the liquid and be transformed into one that picks up dust and polishes at the same time.

Sparkling floors

AS THE floor is the largest surface area in a kitchen, it is important for hygiene that it be brushed and cleaned on a regular basis. In *Good Housekeeping* in the 1950s it was assumed that you would sweep or mop the floor every day. In our busier times this might be difficult to achieve, but with the help of the following advice, it will at least be easier to keep the surface shining.

To keep floor tiles in good condition with the minimum of effort, clean thoroughly and then apply a mixture of beeswax and turpentine. This fills up the pores so that the tiles do not mark or stain easily and they should only require to be washed very occasionally provided care is taken to wipe up spilled liquids as soon as possible. A fresh application of polish should be made weekly or fortnightly, but sparing applications only are required.

Cork Have this flooring 'sealed' with plastic polish or floor seal. Polish weekly with wax polish, and remove any marks or caked polish with steel wool dipped in turpentine.

Linoleum Apply wax polish as above; to build up a good surface, treat first with two coats of water-wax emulsion. Wash with warm soapy water, but avoid scrubbing. Remove marks with steel wool dipped in turpentine.

Quarry tiles Wash with soapy water, and scrub when necessary. Rinse and dry well, so that no grease remains to make the floor slippery. White patches on newly laid tile floors can be washed with a weak solution of vinegar and water. Use a silicone tile polish to 'seal' the surface and help to prevent dirt penetration.

Rubber Polish with water-wax emulsion or special rubber polish. Avoid wax polishes, turpentine or paraffin.

Stone Wash with warm soapy water. Rub down the surface with sandstone brick (or an ordinary brick).

Wood floors Apply wax polish, thinning it with turpentine and using a brush; leave to dry before rubbing up. Remove bad marks by rubbing the way of the grain with medium grade steel wool. A plastic polish or wood seal will give a permanent finish.

EVERYTHING
BUT THE KITCHEN SINK

JUST AS A CRAFTSMAN MAINTAINS THE TOOLS OF HIS trade with loving care, the pukka cook devotes time and attention to keeping kitchen fittings and utensils in mint condition.

Cookers

PASTE CLEANSER and soap-impregnated steel wool pads are useful for removing obstinate marks. Bicarbonate of soda sprinkled on a cold damp cloth will often remove marks from the enamel.

❖

Cooking utensils

STEEP SAUCEPANS immediately after use and wash in hot water, using a stiff saucepan brush or nylon pot scourer to remove any traces of food; avoid harsh abrasives or soda. Stainless steel may, if necessary, be cleaned with steel wool, soap-impregnated pads, or a proprietary steel cleanser.

Use brushes and nylon cleaners rather than harsh abrasives to deal with obstinate particles of food.

To dislodge burnt-on food from a saucepan, fill the pan with water and add a sliced onion and 1 dessertspoon of salt. Boil, then leave to soak overnight; the residue should wash away easily. Or add hot water to the pan with 2 tsp of cream of tartar, simmer for 20 minutes, leave to cool, then rinse and wipe clean. Rubbing a little baking powder into the pan then leaving it overnight can also shift stubborn remnants effectively.

Until a frying pan has become well-seasoned, rub it over with absorbent paper instead of washing.

Soak glass ovenware in cold water, then wash in a hot solution of soapless detergent. Use finest steel wool for removing stains. Rinse thoroughly, or the glass will look cloudy.

Wash baking tins with a hot solution of soapless detergent and dry them thoroughly before putting away. If burnt and blackened, boil up with hot water and washing soda; wash, and finish with an abrasive. To avoid rusting, it is essential to dry tinned ironware very thoroughly; putting them inside a cooling oven is a good way to ensure this.

THE KITCHEN SINK

A GLEAMING SINK IS A SIGN OF GOOD HOUSEWIFERY. As it is such an essential and oft-used feature, see that grime does not build up by using a stiff brush to get well into corners and applying a little paste cleanser if it becomes greasy or marked.

Once a week, fill the sink with hot water and add a few drops of household bleach. Wearing rubber gloves, pull out the plug and replace it upside down. The water will drain away slowly, thoroughly cleaning the overflow, plug holes and the underside of the plug (a neglected area). Rinse well afterwards. From time to time, place a lump of washing soda in the filter and pour over it a kettle of boiling water this will help to prevent the pipe becoming blocked. Rub taps occasionally with half a cut lemon, leave for a few minutes and then wipe dry: this dissolves limescale.

Avoid abrasive, scratchy cleaners for the sink for these will only roughen and spoil it, and result in it staining and becoming extremely difficult to clean. If it should become badly stained, bleaching power mixed into water will usually whiten it effectively.

To whiten a glazed fireclay or porcelain enamel sink, use a mild solution of a proprietary bleach. On no account use the bleach undiluted.

*Q*uick Tips

An easy way to test whether a *cleaning powder* or paste is likely to scratch delicate surfaces is to rub a little between finger and thumb; if particles of sand separate out, this cleaner is too abrasive for anything but heavy scrubbing of wooden tables, draining boards, etc.

Remove obstinate *tea stains* from china by rubbing with salt or borax; a bottle brush may be necessary for dealing with spouts or for getting into awkward corners.

Clean *coffee pots* by pouring in a little water to which ½ tsp of borax has been added. Shake well, rub with a mop and rinse several times.

Remove limescale from a *kettle* by covering the element with equal parts of vinegar and water, then bringing it to the boil. Switch off and leave overnight. Rinse well, then fill with water, boil and empty again before using.

Wash *marble* surfaces with a mild abrasive if necessary. Finish by smearing with a little furniture cream and polish well. Treat stains with paste cleanser or with a little vinegar or lemon juice, but do not allow these acids to remain long, and rinse well. When dry, rub with a drop of salad oil, and polish with a soft duster.

Rub *wooden tableware* occasionally with a rag dipped in a little sweet oil. Wooden fruit and salad bowls should merely be wiped after use (unless stained), as frequent washing tends to dry the wood. To rid chopping boards of strong smells, such as garlic, smear with a paste of bicarbonate of soda and water. Leave for a few minutes, then scrub well and rinse in cold water.

A square of oil-cloth spread in a *dog's or cat's eating place* will often prevent a greasy floor. It is easily removed and cleaned.

To remove white stains from *mahogany* use a little spirit of camphor. Apply it very lightly with a clean soft rag but do not rub it in. Then use a soft duster to polish. Stains caused by hot dishes being put on a table can be instantly removed by this simple method.

A little salt on a damp cloth quickly removes the *brown stains* that appear on egg spoons. The brown particles on the edge of pie dishes can also be removed by scouring with salt.

When antique *ivory* articles become discoloured, they can be polished by rubbing with a mixture of gilder's whiting and water, followed by treatment with a mixture of olive oil and methylated spirit. To finish, polish with a dry cloth.

Prevent mildew developing in a *breadbin* by occasionally wiping it out with a clean cloth wrung out in a solution of vinegar and water (2 tbsp vinegar to 1 pint of water).

CHAPTER EIGHT

Practicalities

*I*n Victorian times, and even well into this century, the most highly prized cooks were those who could not only create magnificent dishes for dinner parties from the finest ingredients, but also help the household accounts by minimising waste, using up leftovers in tasty and satisfying meals. A similar resourcefulness was sought from cooks and maids in prolonging the life of kitchen equipment: floor cloths might be reinforced by sewing 'sides to middle', like sheets, to make them last longer, and the blades of knives were rubbed with mutton suet to prevent rusting. Wartime shortages and rationing in this century prompted new discoveries and examples of ingenuity, and Good Housekeeping shared both its own and readers' tips for ways to 'Keep the Home Front on Active Service'. We can still benefit from these economical or time-saving hints.

MAKING-DO AND MENDING

UNTIL NOT SO VERY LONG AGO, RATHER THAN throwing away broken pieces of china and glass, thrifty housekeepers took pride in expertly mending the most elaborate breaks. Today it tends to be the case that only simple breaks or valuable pieces are mended. Yet preserving is much more rewarding than discarding, and all it takes is care and patience. The advice given below will make it easier still. Use epoxy-based adhesives: quick-setting 'super' glues are only good for very simple breaks, as they leave no time for manipulation.

To mend a wine glass stem

Wash the glass in a mild solution of ammonia and water. Rest it upside down on a flat surface and position the stem. If it won't balance on its own, make a 'collar' from two 38 x 18 mm (1½ x ½ in) rolls of modelling material. Stick one on each side of the bowl, bent around to overlap the break. Apply epoxy adhesive to each broken edge, referring to the manufacturer's instructions. Position the stem between the halves of the collar.

Press the 'collar' on to the stem without letting it touch the joint and so spoil the repair. Press down on the stem to seat it in position. Finally, warm the repair with a hairdryer. Don't let the modelling material melt. Check position of pieces, allow to set and scrape off excess glue.

To mend a simple break in china

Use super glue for simple breaks. Practise fitting the pieces together, as you won't be able to reposition them. Dampen the surface of the break on both pieces to prevent glue being over absorbed. Apply glue to one edge and position the pieces accurately. Press together gently, and remove excess glue with a razor blade or methylated spirits.

❖

To mend a multiple break

USE EPOXY glue (slow-setting if possible) as it will fill up chips and gaps and assemble the pieces in advance of gluing to check for fit.

Mount the largest piece in modelling material and apply glue to the broken edges. Starting at the bottom, stick together the other pieces, one at a time. Press the pieces together as you go. Then support the repair with adhesive tape and warm with a hairdryer for a neat, thin glue line. Let the glue set and remove excess with paint stripper on a rag. Don't take off any glue that is left to fill in chipped edges.

To mend a broken handle

Use epoxy adhesive on handles, even if the break is simple, so you will have time to adjust the fit. If the handle is broken in more than one place, stick it together before attaching it to the main body. Then start with the largest piece and glue the others to it one at a time. When the glue is set, fix on the assembled handle, contacting both ends simultaneously. Then proceed as for multiple breaks. Use adhesive tape to support the handle while the glue sets.

❖

Easing a sticking door

Cupboard doors often stick against their frames. This may be because a loose hinge has allowed the door to drop; or the wood may have swollen, making the door too big; or it may be that the cabinet is standing on an uneven floor. To ease the situation, inspect the hinges and secure loose screws. If there is no fault at the hinge, check the door for signs of abrasion. With the door closed, run a piece of thin paper between the door edge and the frame, noting where it sticks. Sand or lightly plane the points of contact until the door closes freely.

❖

Easing a sticking drawer

Rub a wax candle or beeswax on to the running surfaces of the drawer and in the runners. If the sides of the drawer are swollen, skim areas down with medium sandpaper or a finely set plane. If the drawer still sticks, wax or rub down the front edges. If the runners on the base of the drawer are badly worn, cut strips of plastic laminate. Remove the old runners and glue the strips over them, shiny side down.

KITCHEN KNIVES

WHETHER OR NOT YOU ARE AN ADVANCED COOK OR a novice, knives are essential to a smooth-running kitchen. What *Good Housekeeping* had to say about these utensils in 1956 is just as pertinent today.

If knives are to retain a sharp edge and stand up to hard wear, their blades must be made of good quality steel. The inconvenience of cleaning ordinary steel has made the use of stainless steel almost universal for both kitchen and table knives. It is more difficult to maintain a sharp cutting edge with stainless steel, but this is assisted by the addition of various substances. It is false economy to buy poor quality stainless steel knives, which will soon lose their sharp edges and may also have poor resistance to ordinary household stains.

Even 'stainless' steel can be marked by prolonged contact with some substances, so knives should be washed and dried as soon as possible after use. They can be stained by quite short contact with domestic liquid bleach and by some washing products, including a strong bleach or a sterilising agent; contact with liquid silver-cleaning dips will also tend to blacken stainless steel.

Well-made, sharp-edged kitchen knives lighten many cookery jobs. Scalloped or serrated stainless ones retain their sharpness well, but some people prefer a steel knife for slicing and chopping, as they consider it takes a better edge.

The handle of a knife should be durable and firmly riveted and it is often worth paying a little more in the first instance to get a really strongly made knife.

❖

Storing knives

IF A knife is well cared for and treasured, it will give many years of sterling service. This is how knives used to be kept:

Store knives separately in a case, rack or baize-lined drawer, to retain the sharp cutting edge. If steel knives are put away for any length of time, rub them over with a little petroleum jelly or lanolin and then wrap in paper.

When washing knives with bone handles, avoid immersing the handles because water can split and discolour them. Remove stains from bone handles with a damp cloth dipped in salt, and rub yellowing ivory handles with the cut surface of a lemon.

Sharpening knives

ALL KNIVES require sharpening from time to time.
Whenever you are in doubt about the correct way of
sharpening a knife, it is best to ask the manufacturers or
follow these guidelines.

If you prefer a patent sharpener, buy a well-made one, as
some of the poorer types cause unnecessary wear to the
knife edge. Wheel-type sharpeners are convenient in use,
but tend to give the blade a square edge, which has to be
smoothed off on a stone or steel. A better sharpener has two
revolving steel rods set to the correct angle to give a sharp
edge.

A steel or hone will give very good results for most knives
and is essential for hollow-ground or scalloped-edge types,
which are sharpened by drawing both sides of the blade over
it at an angle of 20 degrees to the steel. Saw-edged knives
cannot be sharpened at home.

To check whether a knife is sharp, hold the edge towards the
light against a dark surface. Any sparkles of reflected light
on the knife indicate blunt areas. If you mislay your
sharpener, knives can be temporarily sharpened by drawing
the blade across the side of a bottle.

Q*uick Tips*

To *untie knots*, place the knot on a table and gently hammer with a wooden spoon or rolling pin several times, turning the knot as you do so. Then insert the closed points of a small pair of scissors, gradually opening them: the knot will come untied.

When one *tumbler* becomes fixed inside another, fill the inner glass with cold water and stand the outer one in warm water. The inner glass contracts and the outer one expands, and in this way they are easily separated.

Pick up splinters of *broken glass* with a wad of cotton wool, then put them in a bin or strong polythene bag.

Repel *flies* by hanging up bunches of basil and mint.

Combat *mice* by scattering cayenne pepper on larder shelves, and plugging mouseholes with balls of brown paper or newspaper dipped in eucalyptus oil.

Hang a small bag near the sink to remind you to put your watches, bracelets and rings in it before *washing up*.

INDEX